SUNSHINE

MORE MEDITATIONS FOR CHILDREN

Other books by Maureen Garth

STARBRIGHT

MOONBEAM

THE INNER GARDEN

SUNSHINE

MORE MEDITATIONS FOR CHILDREN

Maureen Garth

CollinsDove
An imprint of HarperCollins*Publishers*

Published by Collins Dove
A division of HarperCollins*Publishers*
22–24 Joseph Street
North Blackburn, Victoria 3130, Australia

First published 1994

Designed by Pier Vido
Cover design by Pier Vido
Cover illustration by Michelle Ryan
Typeset in Australia by Collins Dove Typesetting
Printed in Australia by Printgraphics Pty Ltd

The National Library of Australia
Cataloguing-in-Publication Data:

Garth, Maureen.
    Sunshine: more meditations for children.

    ISBN 1 86371 406 5.

    1. Meditation — Juvenile literature. 2. Meditations — Juvenile literature. I. Title.

158.12083

For Eleanor, who is my light

Contents

Introduction

Why Children should Meditate

Children are our life blood, our truth, our being, and they are our future. Whatever is put forth to children, by our example, by peer pressure, teachers and media, is going to affect their lives in positive or negative ways. They can easily become confused by conflicting messages. Therefore it is essential to strengthen the positive aspects of life and to give children a safe base within, where they feel secure and where their own truth lies.

Meditation is one way to do this. How lovely it would be if we taught children at an early age how to meditate, to go within, so that they reach their teens and adulthood feeling centered and aware.

And how better to be taught than by you, the parent. Not only will your children benefit from the experience of having you take them through the meditation process, but you too will benefit from the closeness that this special sharing brings.

Most of us think of meditation as being an experience for adults, but it is also one that children can enjoy and which can enrich their lives. Children adapt so well to new experiences. By showing them how to meditate, you are setting up habits which will stand them in good stead throughout their lifetime.

We all want the best for our children. Meditating with your child is a very special way of bonding and sharing of yourself, giving of your time and attention. By this sharing, you are strengthening your child for what lies ahead, giving them security within.

And who could ask for more than a child whose self esteem has been strengthened, who has inner resources, who is centered? That child is our future, our tomorrow.

Because of their receptivity, children are vulnerable to the mixed messages our society offers them. We need to reinforce the messages that can be beneficial to their mind, their heart, and their soul. If the values they learn are positive and life enhancing, they will go into adulthood with strength and a feeling of purpose which should carry them successfully through life. If they succumb to negative values and thinking, they are unlikely as adults to be happy and secure within themselves.

From the time they are born until five years of age, children learn a number of complex things: to focus, to sit, to crawl, to absorb the spoken word, to watch and follow movement, to walk, to speak, to feed themselves, to become miniature self-sufficient adults. Their growth level in that short period of time is nothing short of amazing.

Even before they enter school, children begin to absorb the complex information and techniques that characterize the modern world. Competition can be fierce, even for the youngest school child. There is also the problem of having to make career choices at an early age. Not all children can decide, years in advance, what their chosen vocation will be.

If we make the most of children's receptivity to help them rely upon their inner resources, they will be better equipped to face their future. There are many ways to help children gain inner strength: by parents constantly reinforcing the child's positive attributes; by finding ways to help children to deal with their negative attitudes; by wholeheartedly giving them love and trust; by building their delicate egos; by allowing them self expression; by allowing them to be themselves.

Meditation is one of the ways to achieve all these things. Children need every bit of care and thought we can give them if they are to face the future with strength of mind and purpose.

Meditation is like opening a door which has previously been closed. By opening this door, we invite children to enter into a different way of thought, one that will bring an inner assurance that stays with them throughout their lives.

Meditation can be beneficial for children of all ages. Children are very receptive and can accept new ideas, thoughts, concepts. They see no reason why they should not. They can accept concepts that adults may perhaps find difficult because adults bring the rational mind to bear on any process they undertake. The children's absorption process is different. They may feel they can fly to the moon; adults would look at the difficulties. They may feel there is magic in the air; adults would be practical and say, "What magic?" But for children there is no reason why they cannot fly to the moon or have magic around them, because their minds accept that these things are there for them.

Children have the gift of imagination and I believe we should encourage their minds to grow and to expand by using this gift, which in turn brings forth creativity.

Meditation and imagination go well together. Both allow the child to develop a means of expression that they may not otherwise have. Because children are adaptable, they take to meditation very easily. Sometimes you will notice that your child may appear to be "off" in a different world, one of their own which you cannot enter. Perhaps they are watching an ant taking a crumb too large for its size and struggling to carry it along the path. Children can become totally absorbed in what they are seeing, to the extent they are unaware of anything else. This is a form of day dreaming or meditating.

Children have little difficulty in visualizing a rabbit or a house when you read to them a description from a book. They are often ahead of you and will see in their mind's eye the picture you are drawing with your words. The same thing happens when you take them into the meditative state. Your words invite them to create pictures in their minds.

The meditations in this book are visually rich and excite the child's imagination and creativity. Each meditation takes place within a garden where the children are secure and where nothing can harm them. Each meditation is preceded by the Star Prelude (page 23) which sets up the conditions prior to the meditation. The garden setting is very important because there the children feel secure and are happy to venture upon the meditation experience.

If we teach our children to meditate, they will benefit enormously during their childhood, their youth, and their maturity.

By teaching them to meditate, you are setting up conditions that can help them to be self contained and self assured.

Meditation brings calmness and serenity into our lives. It quietens the mind and the spirit. By teaching our children to meditate, we are giving them a sound base for inner strength and we are setting up a practice which will carry them through their lives, knowing that they will gain knowledge and security of self through their meditation.

Children's Problems

We do not know what worries children because they do not always have the resources to tell us. They may be too young or they may find themselves at a loss to express their feelings, and therefore find it extremely difficult to speak of their concerns. Their behaviour may change and you would be concerned about the reason. The child may say they are OK either because they do not want to talk about the problem, or do not know how to express it.

Within the meditation process, there is a Worry Tree (page 26) which has been extremely helpful to the children who know my books. Before entering the garden and commencing their meditation, they place their worries on the Worry Tree. They can pin their worries there, or just place them on the branches. It is this tree's function to have the worries placed on his many strong branches.

I know of one child (whose parents thought he didn't have a care in the world) who became extremely upset at the thought of placing all his worries on the Worry Tree. He worried about the Worry Tree being able to take all of the worries he was carrying around. So, do we really know what worries children have?

One child lost a grandparent and then a close neighbour who had cared for him. His parents knew he was concerned and upset by these losses and found it helped him to put these concerns on the Worry Tree. The child also started leading the meditations for his parents and told them what worries they had to put on the tree! The family had been going through a difficult time, with a failing business and a consequent move of house, plus personal griefs. Taking his parents through the meditation process and telling them what worries to place on the tree, gave the child a feeling of control over the unhappy conditions that surrounded him.

Another child had lost a family member and she constantly wanted her mother to read the traditional Easter Meditation from my first book, *Starbright*, which says there is no death, and that the spirit lives on. Not surprisingly, it was her favorite meditation because she needed that reassurance. The Worry Tree also assisted her during her grieving process.

Why I Started Meditation with my Daughter

In my first book, *Starbright — Meditations for Children*, I placed a lot of importance on the need to start the meditations as early as possible. I described how I started with my daughter, Eleanor, when she was three years of age, by doing simple visual exercises to quieten her at night. Although she slept well, she had an occasional nightmare. A nightmare is a terrible experience, both for the child and the parent. The child shakes and trembles while the parent wonders what has caused the distress. Is it something he or she has done? What is the child seeing in the waking hours to cause such troubled nights?

Because of my concern, I gave Eleanor a Guardian Angel to make her feel safe. I explained how the wings of the angel would go around her so she would feel protected and secure. I then placed Eleanor in a garden and drew a mental picture for her of what could be in her garden: perhaps lots of animals, perhaps a boat she could climb into, or a cloud to float on.

These exercises grew and grew as time progressed until a theme emerged which I call the Star Prelude. I gave Eleanor a Star and I brought its light down throughout her body; her Guardian Angel was there; I filled her heart with love; I gave her a Worry Tree where she could place anything of concern. Then I would take her into her garden.

Eleanor loved these times so much she wouldn't sleep until I had told her the meditation for the night. It became more than just telling her a story or meditation. We achieved a more complete way of bonding than I had experienced before, and a very beautiful one.

The meditations also tested my skills as a story-teller. I had never considered myself to be imaginative and never a teller of tales, yet, when I sat on the edge of Eleanor's bed, the images flowed. I always started with the Star, the Angel, the heart, the Worry Tree, the entrance to the garden. I would not have any idea what would follow nor what I would say. But when I opened the gate for Eleanor, I always saw something which would give me the story for the night. Sometimes it would be just one thing, say a cloud drifting by. Once I mentioned the cloud, other images would unfold, such as the cloud having reins and coming down to pick her up and take her off into the heavens. I was going into a state of meditation, too, so that the images I saw came from my subconscious.

Eleanor still loves all the meditations that are included in *Starbright* and we have kept on using them, plus the ones in the later books.

I still remember the first time I did the Panda Bear meditation (from *Starbright*) and the look of sheer joy on her face when I described the texture of the fur and how the Panda Bear would give her a big, big cuddle. I did this meditation again a few weeks ago, and there was the same reaction — joy and pleasure. She loves being a fairy — she loves to fly — she loves to be with people — she loves her special garden.

Eleanor was born in July 1981 and I think these meditations will stay with her for years to come. Mind you, I shall certainly be thinking up some new ones for her, but the old ones become like evergreens — always wanted and loved.

In *Starbright* and *Moonbeam* I included a number of meditations I had used with Eleanor and also with many children who had stayed overnight. These children still ask me to do a meditation for them when they stay, even if they have not been with us for some time. And they remember the theme I used before. I find it interesting that, in today's hustle and bustle, the children remember the quiet time they experienced during the meditation and wish to enjoy it once more.

What the Children Say

Here are some comments I received about my first two books *Starbright* and *Moonbeam*, which may be of interest:

Isabella, 2 years old — She put her "itchy bites" (mosquito bites) on the Worry Tree.

Simon, 9 years old — Has always had trouble being settled of a night and sleeping and this is no longer a problem. He is insistent that his mother tell him each evening a meditation which she embroiders according to her own imagination. Now, at the age of 10, he does his own meditation.

Dani and Nicki, 3-year-old twins — They always ask for the books that "draw pictures in the mind".

Phoebe and Jasmine, 4- and 6-year-old sisters — Not only do they insist upon a meditation each evening, but they ensure their parents pack *Starbright* and *Moonbeam* before anything else when they are going on holidays.

Alyson, 8 years old — I met Alyson at a book signing at Santa Cruz in California. She had been using *Starbright* for a year and she drew a picture for me of how she was before and after *Starbright*. The first showed a demented child with hair sticking out at all angles and the second, an angel, with hands crossed, happily in bed.

When the second book, *Moonbeam*, was being tried out at the Eleanora Heights School, some of the comments were:

Claire, 9 years old — When Mrs Moore read the book to us, I felt very relaxed and calm. I liked the story about snow flakes and how we were inside it. It was fun and imaginative and still I felt really settled. I liked the way the writer put the words and how it made me feel.

Clara, 9½ years old — When Mrs Moore read the book to us, I felt safe and calm. It calmed me down a lot. I think the writer was very imaginative. I liked the bit where we were inside the snow flakes and the bit about the beach and how we found the magic ball.

Julianna, 9¾ years old — I have never been to the snow before so the bit about the snow man was really beautiful. It made me feel really relaxed and happy. Once I felt so relaxed I almost fell asleep.

Many adults who have no children, and indeed some who plan to stay that way, tell me they have purchased *Starbright* and *Moonbeam* for themselves. It just goes to show that the child within all of us needs nourishment.

How to Begin

The meditations in this book are, as in *Starbright* and in my second book, *Moonbeam*, only an indication of what you can do. There is no set format. You must feel comfortable with what you are doing and put the meditations into your own words, not mine. The ideas in the meditations might spark off scenes that you might want to explore with your child or children. Whatever I write is for guidance only and to suggest to your subconscious what you could say, not what you should say.

Each meditation starts with the Star (page 23), the focal point for setting up the conditions for the meditation. Indeed, the Star is an integral part, the point where the relaxation and visualization starts. The Star is followed by the Angel — or you might prefer to say a wise person — which in turn can be followed by the Worry Tree (if you feel it is necessary). You then do the meditation you have selected, perhaps the Old Tree or the Purple-winged Bird. Do whatever you feel is appropriate to the mood of the child or children, or even to yourself.

Although I use a Star as the focal point, you might prefer to use the Moon or perhaps the Sun. It does not matter which; the important thing is to give your child something to focus on. For relaxation and visualization, it is as easy to bring the light down from the Sun or Moon as from a Star.

If you use the Moon, for instance, you could say that the Moon's fingers are spreading out over the world so that everyone can see in the night, but there is one special Moonbeam that is coming down just for your child. That Moonbeam is filled with glitter, little sprinkles of which are touching all parts of the body, making it glow in the night.

And if you have selected the Sun, you could speak about how the Sun is a golden ball in the sky, filled with warmth and light. A large shaft of sunshine is dancing down to the child's bed where it is caressing and embracing her or him, filling every part of the body with the Sun's rays. *You* must choose the vehicle with which you feel the most at ease, be it the Sun, Moon, or the Star.

The Tone of Voice

You might think when you read the meditations, that they are not very long. Please remember that when you are speaking, you will do so in a very slow, relaxed voice, pausing to let the scene sink in, so that the child, whose eyes are closed and who is focusing inward, can easily visualize and feel the scene. The way you use your voice is very important. You will find it best to drop your voice by a few tones, speaking more and more slowly, with a soothing quality. There is something hypnotic about a voice which is low and relaxed.

Some of the meditations are longer than others. If you are tired, select a short one. I have found that the children are not concerned with the length, only with the fact that *you* are doing it for *them*.

Although I call them meditations, you might prefer to call them stories. This really is not important, it is only a name. The main thing is that you will be sharing a unique experience with your very special child.

Using the Mind

Using these meditations with children is not the same as reading stories to them. Reading is passive in that the listener follows closely the author's story. Children do understand and become involved when you read a story but, in a guided meditation, they become more actively involved. Reading a story and reading a meditation are different functions. Reading stories to children is a must because it introduces the child to the whole world of literature. It also helps the child to learn to read and spell. But meditation enables the mind to become free, to explore.

Each meditation has its own distinctive theme and gives children the opportunity to experience it. They meet extra-terrestrials; they become a cloud and make cloud pictures; they swim with the mermaid and her family; they travel to the sun with a sun god; they travel the universe; they play a large pipe organ near the Grandfather Tree; they ride horses; they go to the universal library. There are so many things they can do, and all these things must bring their imagination to the fore. They can create these scenes in their minds and feel the sensations they bring. In other words, they participate in the meditation.

For Teachers

I taught meditation at Eleanor's Infant School, which proved to be an interesting experience for several reasons. Very few schools, to my knowledge, encourage meditation. Eleanor's teacher, Helen, who was also the head mistress, said she would like me to introduce meditation as a trial. So, it was a first for me, a first for the children, and a first for the school.

The children were excited when they were asked to sit in a circle in order to meditate. I explained that we were trying something new with them and that meditation was like story-telling, only they would have their eyes closed while I drew a story in their minds.

I did the Star Prelude — the light from the Star, the opening of the heart, the Guardian Angel, the Worry Tree, the garden, and then one of my stories. From the time I started, we noticed that some children immediately went into a relaxed state and stayed motionless for the duration of the meditation. Others fidgeted. They could not sit still and had trouble keeping their eyes closed.

The children who went deeply into meditation, and stayed, happened to be the better students. The ones who fidgeted were children whose attention span was limited and who had difficulty concentrating in the normal course of learning.

Over the next few weeks, I spent time talking with the ones who could not settle. They were not sure what they were supposed to see nor what was expected of them. I explained that they might be able to see, in their imagination, what I was talking about and, if they could not, they might see something else they might want to tell me about.

What surprised both Helen and me was that the children who were having the most difficulty with their studies, were improving. They were able to think processes through, which was not possible before. The quality of their stories improved and showed a far better use of imagination.

At that time, I also helped the children "publish" their stories. They dictated them from their handwritten books and I typed them. Prior to learning meditation, their stories had been about their families, picnics, bikes, etc, with little exercise in imagination, except for the few who naturally visualized well. Again Helen and I were surprised to find that the content of their stories changed and became more colorful, more imaginative, and more creative.

Anything that can free a child's mind should be used. We end up being bound by restrictions, which we must accept to get through life, but our minds should be free and active. Problem-solving becomes easier if the mind can see around corners instead of existing in the limited space to which we sometimes condemn it.

When I do meditations at night, I leave Eleanor at a place in the garden where I feel she will drift into sleep.

In the classroom, you would take the children to a place in the meditation that you feel is right, saying, "I am going to be quiet now and leave you for a while. Let your mind be free. You are very safe and I will bring you back shortly." Leave them in their meditation for approximately five or ten minutes, according to their attention span, then bring them back out of the garden, gently closing the gate behind them. Take them past the Worry Tree, wrap them up in a golden cloak, and tell them to open their eyes when they are ready.

After the meditation, ask each child what they saw or did. You will be surprised at what they come out with. Some see other worlds, some play with animals, some look for the pot of gold at the end of the rainbow (a meditation in *Starbright*). One girl said she saw "space" and described it beautifully. Her classmate, who was very much into intergalactic travel, snorted and said, "Don't be silly, you can't go into space without your space suit and helmet."

Some children have a lot to relate; others are a bit shy of saying anything. If they were meditating for a short time at the start of each day rather than once a week, it would free them up immensely. I understand that if meditation is used prior to study, the study process is easier to assimilate.

The Worry Tree is important for some children who may have many concerns we are not aware of. There could be sibling rivalry, dissension in the home, problems with school friends. How often have we heard that phrase, "I'm not going to be your friend any more", and how often have we had to dry the resultant tears.

Meditation for All

Meditation is a time for reflection and contemplation, a time to go within. It is not beyond the reach of anyone, provided they take the time and create the opportunity.

Meditation is very simple: you need to sit quietly either on your own or with a group of people (it is best to sit in an upright chair — if you make the chair too comfortable, you may fall asleep). Wear loose clothing for comfort but, if that is not possible, loosen anything which is tight around the waist or neck so that you do not feel these restrictions. Try not to cross your arms and legs as this can lead to discomfort.

You might like to have soothing music in the background or you might prefer silence. Sometimes I like to fix a scene in my head, such as the garden in which I place the children. Other times my mind is like a blank screen ready to receive whatever images happen to cross it.

The brain works at different levels of consciousness. These levels are called Beta, Alpha, Theta and Delta. Beta is our normal conscious level, the level at which we work in our daily lives. When we go into a meditative state we are going into Alpha, which enables us to create scenes and images on the screen of our mind. There are also the levels, Theta and Delta, which we can attain as we go more deeply into the meditative state. Delta is our sleep level. Most of us work very well within Alpha, and come back feeling refreshed and renewed.

It is up to the individual to decide how long to spend in meditation. If you can only spare five or ten minutes that can be ample. To feel the full benefit however, twenty minutes is better because meditation can promote calmness, relax tension, and give relief from anxiety as you become detached from your problems. Your problems will not necessarily go away, but meditation can be beneficial to the way you handle those problems. Sometimes the solution comes when we take the time to sit quietly.

Meditation is a very soothing, relaxing way of coping with the stress and anxiety of daily life. Many doctors recommend meditation as a wise and good practice for their patients. It is a relaxing and pleasant way to spend such a short period of time, and one that has many benefits.

The Star Prelude

I WANT you to see above your head a beautiful, beautiful Star. This Star is very special to you as it is your very own Star. It can be any color you like — you might see it as being a purple star, or perhaps a pink one — or blue — or yellow — or is it a speckled star? Or a silver one? Because it is your very own Star, it can be any color or colors you choose.

This special Star is filled with white light, lovely white light which shimmers and glows. I want you to see this light streaming down towards you until it reaches the very top of your head. And now I want you to bring this pure light down through your head and take it right down your body until your whole body is filled with this glorious white light.

I want you to feel the light going down your arms, right down, until you feel it reaching your hands and going into each and every finger.

Feel that light going down the trunk of your body, down until it reaches your legs, and when you feel it there, take it right down until it comes to your feet and then feel the light going through each toe.

I now want you to look into your heart and to fill your heart with love for all the people and animals in the world. They are your friends, be they large or small. Can you see your heart getting bigger and bigger? It's expanding because you have so much love in your heart for all these people and the animals, and of course for yourself.

Now your Guardian Angel is waiting to wrap golden wings of protection around you before taking you into your garden. The Angel's wings are very large and very soft, just like down. Everyone has their own Guardian Angel and that Guardian Angel takes care of you and protects you always, so you are never alone. It's important to remember this and to know that you have someone who looks after you with love and care.

Your Guardian Angel is now going to take you to a garden which is your own special place, but before you enter I want you to look at the large tree which is outside. This tree is called the Worry Tree. I want you to pin on this tree anything which might worry you — perhaps you have had some arguments at school, or maybe you are having difficulty with your school work. This tree will take any worries at all, be it with your friends or your family. This tree accepts anything that you would care to pin there.

Your Guardian Angel is now opening the gate for you to enter and, as you go in, you find the colors are like nothing you have seen before. The beauty of the flowers, the colors, the textures and the perfume — breathe them in. The grass is a vivid green and the sky a beautiful blue with little white fluffy clouds. It is very peaceful in your garden; it is full of love and harmony.

> You may feel this prelude is very long but it is wise to create with care, thought and feeling the scene your child is entering. When your child is used to it, the prelude may become shorter, as it is not always necessary to describe the Star and the Angel in such full detail. Then it becomes something like the shorter version below.

I want you to see above your head a beautiful, beautiful Star. This Star is filled with lovely white light. I want you to bring the white light from that Star right down through your body until you can feel it in every part of your body, and your heart is filled with love for all humanity and for all creatures great and small.

Your Guardian Angel is waiting to wrap a golden cloak of protection around you and take you to the Worry Tree. Put anything which worries you on the tree and then your Guardian will open the gate and take you inside your garden.

Your garden is filled with glorious flowers, the grass and the trees are an emerald green, and the sky a deep blue with white clouds.

After you have set the scene, as it were, you can do anything with the children that you think they would enjoy. Become a child again yourself — I think you will be surprised at what pleasure these flights of fantasy will give you.

The meditations that follow in this book and those in my other two collections, *Starbright* and *Moonbeam*, have been done for children of all ages. I have incorporated different themes that I feel will appeal to both the adult and the child. Indeed, some of these meditations you may care to use for yourself, along with those in my collection for adults, *The Inner Garden*.

Sunshine

YOUR GARDEN is lit by the light of the sun as you
enter. The animals are coming forward, their fur
warm from the sun's rays, and the feathers of the
birds move in the light breeze that drifts through
your special garden. The flowers stand tall and strong
in the sunlight, sending their beautiful perfume
through the trees and the bushes nearby.

The sun's rays dapple lightly through the trees, lighting some sections of the grass and flowers, leaving others in the shade so the plants and the animals can experience the coolness from the shade and then step into the shaft of the sun, welcoming its warmth. Feel the light of the sun surrounding you, warming your body, allowing you to feel good.

All the animals love having the sun's light surrounding them. They luxuriate in its warmth, and they stretch their limbs slowly as they awaken from their sleep on the rich green grass.

Some animals have been lying on rocks which have taken the sun's warmth deep within. These animals will feel the glow and warmth coming from these rocks long after the sun has disappeared.

The butterflies have come in all their wondrous colors, moving in the sunshine which dapples through the trees. Some butterflies have wings which are a rich blue and very large, with a lighter blue making an intricate pattern. Some are small and pure white except for their black eyes and feelers. There are others that are orange with black tracings on their wings. And there are many more of different colors and patterns which glow as they move in the sunshine.

Feel yourself walking along your pathway, the sun's gentle fingers falling across your body. The sunshine is lighting your garden in a special way. The sun's rays go deep into the earth, helping the plants and grass to grow, and everything you see around you seems to glow in its light.

You may care to lie down on the grass, which feels like velvet beneath you, and to have the sunshine drift across your body, warming you and making you feel good inside.

While you lie there, surrounded by the sun's light, you may find a special ray of sunshine coming towards you. This ray is yours and will always surround you when you think of the sun and the sun's world which is different to ours.

Lie there and feel the sunshine, which has been surrounding you, lifting you up as though to cradle you, so that you can go high into the heavens where the sun's light comes from. You feel comfortable and at ease with its light and warmth, and this special ray of sunshine is very gentle and loving as it takes you above the earth. You may want to drift upwards so that you can see the beams of light that criss-cross the earth, bringing life and warmth to all in their path.

Your ray of sunshine may travel down one of these beams above your own home, showing you how its light and warmth streams into your house and touches each person who lives there. Or perhaps your ray of sunshine may take you to a large waterfall whose waters gleam in the sun's light, its droplets flying through the air like diamonds, before landing on the warm rocks and disappearing.

Your ray of sunshine could take you wherever you want to go …

The Old Tree and his Friends

THE AIR is fresh and ruffles your hair as if a hand is playing with it. The sun is sending its golden rays down, lighting up the branches on the trees and placing a glow around all that it touches. The flowers are sending out their beautiful perfume and are nodding as if to greet you as you enter your garden.

You may want to pick some flowers as you go

further into your garden. When you pick them, other flowers appear in their place, as nothing ever dies in your special garden. You can pick as many flowers as you want, flowers of all colors and types. The rose thorns will not prick your fingers because the thorns disappear as soon as the roses are picked. You could make a small posy if you like and carry them with you as you go further down the pathway.

The animals are coming from everywhere. I wonder where they are going? There are animals of all descriptions, some small, some large. There are bandicoots, jaguars, zebras, lions, elephants, rabbits, and even some gazelles.

Birds of all types are flying fast, dipping and swirling in the air. There are doves, swallows, sea gulls, and even some eagles with their very large wing span.

One of the lions is stopping for you to hop on her back so that you can travel with the animals. She is very strong and her paws thud as they hit the earth. She flies like the wind. The air is catching your hair and throwing it every which way.

The lion is slowing down now and the other animals are catching up. The birds are coming to land on the branches of a very old gnarled tree. All the animals are coming to rest around his trunk, and the tree is waving his branches in welcome. This is the Grandfather Tree. He is the oldest tree in your garden, and he has a lot of wisdom and love. The animals love to rest beneath his branches, leaning against his trunk, and the birds like to nestle on his branches, feeling the leaves brush against their feathers.

The Grandfather Tree is holding out a branch in welcome. He would like you to sit close to his trunk on the large root that goes forth into the earth. Can you see who is peering around his trunk? It is one of the prettiest fairies whose wings are lightly touched with pink and her dress is of silver. She has a large bow in her hair. With her is a small elf dressed all in green, and his hat sits at an angle over his left eye and his boots turn up at the toes.

If you look behind the tree, you will find there are many more fairies and elves, all coming forward to meet you.

The Grandfather Tree is so happy that you have come to share this time with the animals, the birds, and the little people. He loves children to sit close by his strong trunk which holds his many branches high in the air.

The fairies and the elves are playing lovely music and you may feel like dancing with one of the animals, or by yourself. Or you may feel like sitting with the Grandfather Tree and watching the others …

Shooting for the Stars

AS YOU enter your garden, you can feel the freshness of the night air caressing your cheeks, ruffling your hair, surrounding your body. The flowers are bending their bodies in the slight breeze as though to say something is going to happen.

There is an air of excitement in your garden, an air that says you are going to travel far, far away, perhaps even out of this world. Would you like that? Some people say they are going to shoot for the stars and perhaps you could do the same. Have you thought about going to the stars? I think that would be fun.

Just stand in the clearing in the centre of your garden, near the Grandfather Tree, and turn your face upwards towards the many stars that are in the sky overhead. They are all sending a lovely light down to where you are in your garden. Look at all the stars and you will find that one will stand out from the rest with its beautiful light. This is the one that you will go to.

Keep looking towards the star you have chosen and you will see a stream of brilliant white light coming towards you. This white light is like a link of energy which will transport you forever upwards. You can feel your body lifting off the grass and being taken high above the earth moving towards the heavens. It is lovely to feel free and to be transported by this pillar of light. The air is fresh and cool around you and the many stars in the universe sparkle in the black velvet sky and send off many twinkling lights which can be seen on the earth.

This beam of light is taking you faster and higher as you shoot past many smaller stars. And there you are, standing on the star you have chosen. This star's light streams towards the earth.

Look at the star earth beneath your feet and you will find it very different than what you normally stand on. It is full of small sparkles which light the path you are on and show the way. There is a waterfall nearby and, if you stand underneath it, you will find that instead of water coming around your body, you are being bathed in special starlight so that you now sparkle and gleam with this lovely starlight.

You may find star people living here. I wonder what they will look like? I imagine they will have wonderful silver clothes and flowing hair. They may speak a different language but you will be able to understand them. Why don't you go looking for them? I think they would love to know someone has traveled such a long way to see them …

The Mermaid and her Family

YOUR GARDEN has a lovely feel to it as you enter and it seems to greet you. The flowers bend from their waists and nod, and butterflies of many different colors crowd around the lilies and daffodils.

As you go further forward into your garden, you can hear water splashing and the sound of laughter. I wonder where this can be coming from?

How beautiful the water is as you turn the corner and the sea comes into view. The sand is bright from the sun gleaming down and the water looks so clean and fresh and blue. If you walk along the beach a little way, you will come to a cove which is small and protected, and this looks like a very special place where you can swim.

There are large rocks in the crystal clear water and small fish of many varied colors swim around them. Why don't you dive into the water and swim with the fish? They would love to float in the water with you. These fish are all the colors of the rainbow and of many different shapes and sizes.

I can see a movement deep in the water. Why don't you dive into the depths to see where this

movement is coming from? If people do live
underneath the water, they must have a lovely home
so deep beneath the sea. Can you see who it is?
I think they are playing games with you.

Why don't you come back to the surface of the
water and sit on one of the rocks? There is a large
rock nearby and someone is sitting there. She has
lovely long hair which she is combing out for the sun
to dry, and a very long tail. Why, it is a mermaid.
I wonder what it would be like to be a mermaid?
She is smiling and laughing at you and beckons you
to come closer.

She has very white teeth and a beautiful smile as
she makes you welcome. If you look at the other
rocks coming out of the water, you will see there are

mermaid children resting on these rocks and waving to you.

The mermaid would like to take you to her home, which is a cave underneath the water. The children on the other rocks are preparing to dive as she takes you by the hand before gently leaving her rock.

She is taking you deep under the water and into the cave where her husband, the merman, is. He has prepared a great feast in your honor and they would love you to join them for a seaweed dinner.

The children are all giggling and are so happy that you have come to see them. They have a spare tail for you to put on so that you can feel what it is like to swish it around as you dive through the water.

It is such fun to swim with this lovely family. You may want to swim back to the rocks later and watch the ships go by. Perhaps you could wave to the people and surprise them by swishing your new tail at them …

Traveling in a Balloon

THE AIR feels fresh and clean against your skin and you can feel the gentle breeze ruffling your hair as it moves through your garden.

Flowers of many colors are sitting tall and proud, happy to share their beauty with you. The earth has been absorbing the sun's rays and feels warm beneath your feet.

Some of the animals that share your garden are coming forward to greet you and they seem to be excited. The ruffle of fur sits proudly around the lion's head as he walks over to you, roaring his welcome. There are rabbits coming out from their burrows, twitching their whiskers. A small monkey is pulling at your sleeve as though to ask you to hurry to the Grandfather Tree.

This old tree has many birds nestling amongst his branches, some of them fluffing out their feathers as they settle down. Others are feeding the little ones in their nests where they are protected and secure.

The Grandfather Tree is moving his branches, his green leaves rustling as though to welcome you. The monkey is climbing up his thick trunk and onto a branch where she is excitedly pointing to something in the clearing.

Why, it is a huge balloon with a small wicker basket hanging underneath. The balloon has purple, pink, mauve and yellow stripes which narrow at the top and bottom, and swell out in the centre. These colors are very vivid and stand out strongly against the deep blue sky. The sun is sending its warmth down and its light is picking up the colors, making them appear luminescent.

Why don't you get inside the basket? You will find that it is larger than it appears from the outside and quite comfortable. The balloon is high above you and is beginning to move in the gentle breeze. The North Wind is coming forward and asking if you would like him to blow gently around the balloon so that you can go not only high into the air, but travel across the fields.

This balloon is operated by a small lever which is set in the wicker basket. Push this lever gently forward and the balloon will lift off from the earth and float into the heavens.

The Grandfather Tree is shaking his branches in farewell and the birds are leaving his branches to fly with you. The animals are sitting in the clearing to wait for your return.

Around the inside of the basket there is a padded seat covered in purple satin. A large yellow bow is attached to some of the struts which hold the basket to the balloon, and the tails of the bow are streaming behind you as the wind pushes you further.

This balloon can take you wherever you want. You can go high into the air, higher than you have been before, or you could ask the Northerly Wind to breathe gently on the balloon and its basket, turning you in a spiral.

Whenever you want to land, all you have to do is to pull the lever back and you will find your descent will be gentle, with a slight bump as you come to the earth.

I wonder where you have landed? You may have come back to the Grandfather Tree and the animals, or you may have gone to another city, another place, another country …

The Magic Hat

THE FLOWERS are pushing their heads forward to catch the sun's golden rays. You can hear the light breeze rustling through the leaves of the many trees that are in your garden. There is much excitement as you enter your garden. The birds are flying swiftly in one direction and the rabbits, emerging from their burrows, are bounding past you, their feet making a definite thud as they hit the earth. Why don't you follow them to see where they are going?

It is rather hard to keep up with them as they are so fast, but they are now slowing down for you. One of them is taking you by the hand, so that you feel as though your feet fly across the earth as you run with the rabbits.

The rabbits have all stopped and are pointing to a small three-legged stool in front of the Grandfather Tree. A very large hat is sitting in the centre of the stool and it would seem as though it has been left there for you.

The hat is bright green with small slashes of yellow through it. The hat's brim is wide and has a multi-colored ribbon around it, with a large bow on one side. Why don't you put it on? I believe it is a magic hat and that when you put it on, you will be able to do all sorts of tricks to entertain the rabbits and the other creatures that are coming forward.

Look, now that you are wearing the hat, you can pull cards out from behind the ribbon and also from your sleeves. There is a long scarf appearing from the brim which you can tie underneath your chin if you want.

Why don't you take the hat off and look inside? Why, there is a pretty white dove inside and I do believe she has laid an egg. You can hold her in your hand if you like and, if you hold the egg in the other hand, it may even hatch.

You can have such fun with this hat. It can make

you disappear if you want. Put it on and **"wish"** yourself invisible. When you do that, you can move around and no one can see you. What fun!

This special hat can also transport you wherever you want to go. If you want to visit a special person, you could put it on and travel there in no time. You may want to see a friend, or perhaps travel to another country. This hat could take you to Disneyland where you could meet some of the Disney characters or to the North Pole where you could slide on the ice and perhaps meet Santa and Mrs Claus.

This is such a lovely magic hat. When you put it on, it makes you feel happy and you want to laugh when you wear it. And why don't you laugh, because this hat makes you feel so good …

Being a Cloud

AS YOU enter your garden, you can smell the wonderful perfume the flowers are sending forth and their aroma drifts around you. The sky is a rich beautiful blue and the soft green grass glistens with the dew that has been left by the early morning mist.

Why don't you lie down, feeling the soft green grass beneath you, and watch the clouds drifting across the beautiful blue sky?

There seem to be many clouds in the sky. If you watch carefully, you will notice that the clouds appear to make faces and forms that you have not noticed before. I wonder how the clouds do that?

Why don't you step onto your own personal small cloud which has come down into the clearing? It has a small red seat which will hold you comfortably, and a set of golden reins. Your cloud will take you high above the earth, into the heavens above. Can you feel the cloud lifting off from the clearing? Grandfather Tree is waving his branches at you and some of the birds are flying alongside your cloud.

You are going higher and higher, leaving the earth behind. Your cloud is weaving in and out of some of the other clouds as it takes you to Mother

Cloud where it will stop.

You can get off on Mother Cloud and talk to the cloud people if you like. Jump up and down and feel the softness of the cloud supporting you and your weight. You could then hop from one cloud to another without falling, as the law of gravity is different on the clouds.

Why don't you take part of a cloud and make it into a shape like your mother or father? You can use the cloud to make faces of other family members, perhaps your brother or sister, or maybe you would like to make faces and bodies of animals.

You could have one cloud with a whole family of cats. Perhaps a small cat with her little ones, or you may like to make a lion and her cubs.

Some clouds are small and wispy. You could collect them all together and form them into one cloud. You could push and pull here and there until you get the cloud to the size you want. And then you could make special faces with the cloud you have formed.

Over there is a cloud that looks as though it could rain. Why don't you move that cloud to a part of the earth that looks as though it needs rain, and then push the cloud gently so that the rain falls. If you hang on under the cloud, you can have a shower at the same time.

Perhaps there are other clouds with rain that you could move around, or maybe you may like to make more cloud people …

The Green Train

THE SUN hangs overhead like a rich golden globe, filled with a warm light which is bathing you in its gentle glow, and the freshness of the air brushes your face lightly. The sky is a rich sapphire blue hung with the merest wisps of cloud.

There is a feeling of something different in your garden, as though something is going to happen.

Listen carefully, and see what you can hear.

I can hear the whistle of a train. Can you? Listen, it is tooting as it comes around the bend. What a marvellous train, so green and shiny. There is smoke coming out as the engine driver pulls the cord to make it toot.

It is now pulling into the station. Why don't you hop on board and go for a ride? You never can tell where this train will take you. This is a mystery train that can take you on many different adventures, to many different places.

You can wander from carriage to carriage as the train sways on its tracks, still tooting occasionally, and the wheels make sounds as though they are talking to you as they turn. Can you hear what they are saying?

Listen carefully, as the wheels pass their message along.

Each carriage is done in different colors and different themes. Some carriages seem as though they are from the Wild West. Others are from the future and their seats are made of different materials. And others are from different times in our past. You may want to go back one hundred years or perhaps forward by two hundred years. Or you may want to stay in your own present time.

Some carriages have beds which you can hop into if the journey is very long. The beds feel very comfortable as the train makes its way, moving gently around the bends.

If you are hungry, you can always go to the dining car where they have all sorts of food from many different countries.

You could go to the front of the train and meet the driver. I am sure the driver would like to show you how to blow the whistle and to make the train go slow as it rounds the corners, and then to pick up speed when it is on the straight.

Why don't you sound the whistle for the driver? You can make the sounds long or short, or perhaps a little of each. I know, why don't you see if you could be the train driver for a little while. Because this train goes on mystery tours, it would be fun for you to be the driver and see where you will be taken. I am sure you can find a hat to fit you …

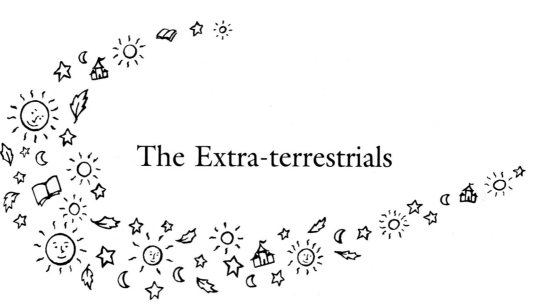

The Extra-terrestrials

THE SKY is clear and the warmth of the sun radiates to where you are in your garden. The trees are whispering to each other and they are pointing you towards the mountains in the distance.. The mountains are tall and graceful as they stand outlined against the blue of the sky, and they have small white caps on their peaks.

There seems to be something sparkling in the valley at the base of the mountains. It is catching the light from the sun and it makes you want to investigate, to see what is causing this reflection of light.

Have you ever wondered about people from other planets and other time zones? I think that sometimes extra-terrestrials visit us on earth but they do not always show themselves to us. They like to keep to themselves as not all people would understand why they have come from their homes which exist in a land or planet so far removed from ours.

I think you might find a space ship close to the mountains, which is why the light is being reflected from the sun's rays.

Can you see the ship now? It is large and silver and has several antennae sticking out and shines in the sunlight. These antennae are their receiving station and their connection with their mother ship and the planet they call home. I think you will find that the people on this intergalactic craft have traveled to earth just to meet you.

There are stairs being lowered from the main body of the aircraft and there is an extra-terrestrial at the top who beckons for you to come forward and into the body of the craft. Go up the stairs and greet your new friend by extending your hand in welcome.

Can you see what your friend looks like? People from space do not always look as we do, but that doesn't matter. Take the hand being offered to lead you inside. There are several space people in the craft and they are going to take you around and show you how the craft moves through space.

The interior of this vehicle is very different than our airborne craft. Their computer equipment is smaller and easier to operate and the equipment is white, except for the flashing lights. If you sit at the controls, you will notice that the wide windows go completely around the craft, enabling you to see not only in front, but around the sides and the back as you turn.

I wonder whether they would allow you to operate the controls. Would you like to take off and go to where they live? If you ask, perhaps they will allow you to do so. I am sure they will think it a wonderful idea ...

The Universal Library

THE SLIGHT wind moves through your hair and the air is fresh and cool as you enter your garden. White clouds silently float above and the sun's gentle warmth falls like a light mantle around you. There are also wisps of clouds in the blue sky overhead and the leaves from the trees create a soft carpet for you to walk on.

The flowers are in full bloom and the smell of the roses floats towards you making you feel as though you would like to pick one. The roses are abundant in their assorted colors of yellow, white, pink, red and deep purple. Their colors complement the green shrubs and trees that stand guard, protecting them from the sun when it is high in the heavens.

Through the trees, you can see the outline of a large building which is made of alabaster with tall sculptured columns around it.

There are many stairs to climb before you reach the heavy wooden doors which are ornately carved. There are words written above these doors and they say, "The Universal Library". Why don't you go inside and see what this building has to offer?

The entrance hall is large and imposing and its marble floors have an intricate pattern as though the solar system has burst forth. There are many marble statues and busts of learned scholars on stands scattered throughout this hall and also in the halls that lead in different directions.

There are rooms down each hallway that you could enter and each one is filled to the ceiling with books. To get to the ones at the top, you need to climb a ladder which then slides from one wall to the other.

There are books on every subject you could imagine and also books on those that you couldn't.

Each room deals with different subjects. Some rooms have books which are on space travel and the universe. Others are filled with stories about different cultures and people of the earth. And some are stories about families, about children, about animals. And some are about people who dare to do things — who climb mountains, who build aeroplanes, who travel to distant lands. Some rooms tell us all about the history of the world and our people, with rooms that tell us about the many animals that live on earth. And other rooms deal with our history, going back to the time of the dinosaurs and when people first trod the earth.

I wonder which room you will choose. You may want to spend only a little time in one, and then move on to the next. There are so many books that are interesting. It is up to you to decide …

The Fun Park

THERE IS an air of excitement as you enter your garden. I wonder what can be causing it? The flowers are bending their heads towards each other and the trees are waving their branches in welcome in the light breeze. The many birds sitting on the branches are twittering and preening themselves.

You can hear a lot of chattering as you go down your pathway. Listen carefully to find out where this noise and activity is coming from and then head in that direction.

Why, in the clearing, there is a fun park with lots of rides. There are some rides that take you high in the air and spin you around. This makes you laugh as you find yourself upside down for a short time before being put upright once again. Afterwards, when you first put your feet back on the earth, you may find yourself a bit wobbly from being turned around so many times.

And then there are small cars which you can drive around and around, and sometimes crash into others that are also going in the same direction.

Because of the padding around the outside of the cars, no one ever gets hurt.

There are large slippery dips where you feel yourself sliding down and down, and the mat underneath you goes from side to side. You laugh, loving the feeling of the downward motion, until you hit the bottom, and then you want to go back to the top to do it all over again. If you carry your mat back with you, there is no reason why you cannot come down as many times as you want.

And then there is the merry-go-round, which is beautifully painted and has mirrors which will reflect both you and the horse you have chosen as you go round and round. Perhaps you could choose the white horse with the long, flowing mane who looks as though she wants to take off, or maybe the black one that is prancing high in the air. The merry-go-round plays music as you ride your horse around, going up and down all the while.

There are games that you can play where you throw balls into the mouth of the clown as the head turns from side to side. This can be difficult as sometimes the ball just misses. If you concentrate, I am sure you will get the balls in.

On that stall in front of you they are playing darts. I wonder if you can get all your darts into the bull's eye? If you do, I am sure you will win one of their prizes.

I wonder where else you could go? There are so many things you could do here …

The Purple-winged Bird

THERE ARE many birds flying around your garden, landing on the branches of the green trees and bushes that surround you. The bees are busy humming as they fly from flower to flower collecting their pollen, and the butterflies fly past in a burst of color which is like a rainbow.

The Grandfather Tree seems to be smiling to himself. I wonder why? I think he has someone special sitting on one of his branches. This wise old tree is lowering one of his limbs for you to climb on and is now taking you up into the air, placing you on a branch that is high so that you can see all around.

In the distance you will see a small shape flying, making for the protection of the Grandfather Tree's branches. As she becomes closer, you will see she is a very different bird and also a very beautiful one. In fact, she is a brilliant purple bird and her name is Parthia.

Her beak is sky blue and the feathers on her body are a rich purple. The crest of her head has blue feathers which match the color of her beak. If you look at her feet, you will notice the claws are a brilliant yellow.

Would you like to be brightly colored like Parthia, or would you like to have your own colors? If you were a bird, perhaps you might have bright green wings with a yellow beak and orange nails. Or you might like to be pure white with a tinge of color on the crest of your head and your nails might be bright red.

Parthia has a twinkle in her eye and a good sense of humor. She likes to have the company of children when they visit this special part of their garden, and if you ask, she may teach you how to fly.

Parthia follows the winds and listens to them as they tell tales of what is happening in other parts of the garden. She loves to sing and has the most beautiful singing voice you have heard. If you listen closely, you too may be able to sing like her.

Why don't you allow Parthia to teach you how to fly, to take off from your high branch and to soar, to dip and weave in the air, perhaps even flying in circles for a time?

The winds are telling Parthia that they will help to carry both of you on your journey. They will breathe behind you as you fly, giving a small push through the air and the clouds, taking you further than you have been before.

Why don't the two of you take off from the Grandfather Tree, and feel the freedom of flight, with the winds helping you along the way? Listen closely

to the winds and to Parthia, the purple-winged bird,
as you travel through the air. Listen, and fly ...

The Clown

THE GRASS is cool beneath your feet and the trees are tall and in full leaf. The breeze gently ruffles their branches and moves lightly through your hair as you walk down your pathway.

There is a lot of excitement in your garden. Can you feel it? The trees are shaking their branches and the flowers are nodding their heads as you pass by. I wonder what is happening? You will have to go further down the path to find out. I hear laughter and I am sure that when you walk around that big tree down there, you will find out where this is coming from.

There is someone waiting for you in your garden, someone who is all dressed up, someone who is ... a clown!

His shoes are very big for his small feet. They look as though he may fall over if he tries to walk, but he doesn't. You look at his feet and want to laugh as his shoes look so odd. Big and red with orange bows. And his clown suit is not only large and floppy but is colored in bright checks of green, yellow, gold and orange. Look at his makeup. A very large bright red mouth has been painted over his own, and his face is chalk white.

This clown is going to take you by the hand. He wants you to go with him into the clearing where a crowd of people are waiting for his performance. They have been waiting for both of you.

He has many balls that he is going to juggle. It looks very easy, doesn't it? He wants someone to be his assistant and is asking you to come forward and help. Would you like to do that?

He is going to a suitcase he has near a tree and is pulling out a small clown's costume with a pair of silly shoes and a crazy hat for your head. Why don't you get dressed up and perform with this clown? I wonder what his name is?

He is jumping up and down in front of the

people doing cartwheels. He is beckoning to you to do the same and he also wants to play leap frog.

He now has a small red wheelbarrow with brown wheels and green spokes. He wants you to get inside so he can wheel you around the arena. He is jerking the wheelbarrow as he goes around, which makes the crowd laugh. And now he wants to get into the wheelbarrow so that you can wheel him around. His legs hang over the sides and his funny shoes stick up into the air.

Why don't you try to juggle the balls? There are six of them of different colors and it seems easy enough to get them all into the air at the one time. You could even throw one into the audience for them to throw back to you …

The Universe

THE GRANDFATHER Tree is looking especially beautiful in the moonlight. The light breeze is drifting through his branches, rustling his green leaves, and the sound is like music. Your garden is very quiet and still and the flowers have tilted their heads back to receive the light from the many stars above which is bathing your garden. This light streams down, mingling with the light from the full moon which hangs in the sky.

Why don't you lie down and look at the stars above you? There are many stars with many names. You could even name some of the stars for yourself and your family if you like. There are some that appear larger and brighter than others because they are bigger, or closer to the earth. Others twinkle from far, far away, sending out a smaller light.

Some stars form a wide pathway as though they have traffic passing along them, while others stand alone, on a solitary path. People who visit the stars would need a special trip to these solitary stars.

You may see a pattern within the stars and perhaps you will want to go beyond that star pattern to see what else is out there.

The universe is wide and deep and holds many mysteries and many planets. We know of planets such as Mercury, Venus, Mars, Jupiter, Saturn, Neptune, Uranus, Pluto and Chiron, but there are many that have not been discovered yet.

Why don't you visit the planets that no one knows about? There is a star coming down to where you are in your garden. It is landing alongside for you to enter the small door which is opening from its centre. This star will take you far, far away, high into the velvet sky. You can see out from this star as it takes you above the earth and you can see the light it emits as it takes you along a different pathway in the sky.

You could circle the universe in this star or you could go further into the other galaxies of which we know so little.

Look, there is a large planet ahead. It is hanging in the sky and looks so different to our planet, Earth. I wonder if you will find people and animals living there like the ones at home. They may be quite different to anyone you have known or seen but I am sure that if you greet them in a friendly fashion, they will make you welcome.

Would you like to land on this large planet, or would you like to go further into the universe to see what other mysteries this particular galaxy may hold before moving on to the others ...?

The Lion who Roared

YOU CAN feel the peace and harmony in your garden. The sky is an indigo blue and the clouds are small and scattered. The sun is a rich golden yellow and spreads light dappling through the trees.

The birds are twittering, the rabbits hopping, the lions roaring, the squirrels are running up the trees with the nuts they have gathered, and the monkeys swing through the branches as you enter your garden. There are dogs and cats and elephants, camels and boldly colored parrots, all waiting to greet you.

A small monkey is approaching you. Why don't you offer her a banana? Look, she is holding out her hand as she wants to take you to a place which is deeper in your garden.

Perhaps you could swing through the trees, as the monkey does, holding onto branches and vines which will take you from one tree to another.

Your monkey is pausing to point to the rock below where a lion is slumbering. This lion is very strong and has a beautiful golden coat which is sleek and shines in the sunlight. Watch as she stretches her body as she awakens from her sleep. The legs go tight and then relax as she sits on her haunches.

The rock she is standing on is high above a valley and this lioness is surveying the territory around as though she owns it. She is now opening her mouth and letting out a magnificent roar which is resounding through the valley and the trees.

You will notice that other animals are responding to the roar. The lion sends her magnificent voice out not once but three times, in quick succession. I think she is summoning the animals to her side.

Your monkey is climbing down the tree and is pausing just above the lion's head, before leaping down to the rock. The monkey is now inviting you to join them. It is an easy climb down the tree to the rock and, if you rest a little every now and again, you will soon find yourself standing beside the monkey, looking straight into the tawny eyes of this mother lion.

Her mouth is opening wider and wider, and the roar that comes out seems to bounce from the trees and around the valley. This is her roar of welcome. Could you roar like the lion? I believe you can. Let your lungs fill with air, and then … roar! What a marvellous sound you have made. The lion is padding over to stand alongside you and both of you can roar together, alerting all the animals to come forward.

As you roar together, look around and you will find animals of all descriptions coming to where you are on the rock. All these animals co-exist peacefully and they love coming together, especially when they have a new guest.

Have you wondered what it would be like to be a lion? Perhaps you could **"wish"** yourself into the body of a lion so that you can see through tawny eyes. Doesn't it look and feel different now that you are a lion? Roar, and let all the animals know that you are there ...

The Traveling Armchair

THERE IS a hushed air of expectancy in your garden as you enter. The animals are sitting close to the trunks of the many trees and the flowers are waving their heads, creating a rainbow of color, as they send their beautiful perfume forth to drift around you.

The sun is sending out gentle rays to where you are and the trees move gently with the light breeze.

There is a small hill in front of you and, sitting on its top, is an armchair. What a strange place to find an armchair!

It is a very large chair with bold stripes of green and yellow going down its sides. It has overstuffed arms and a heavily padded back which makes it look extremely comfortable. The red tassels which hang from the arms swing in the slight breeze and, around its base, is a skirt with green and yellow stripes going in the opposite direction.

It looks very comfortable, the sort of armchair that you can snuggle down into. Why don't you climb onto the seat and pull the red tassels hanging from its arms? As you do so, a set of controls comes out in front of you from either side, and they meet in the center so that you have a control panel across your lap.

This is a very unusual armchair because it is a traveling one. Why don't you press the "go" button and see what happens?

The armchair shudders slightly as it prepares for take off, and then moves silently into the air, hovering for a short while above the hill as it awaits your commands.

This armchair will take you wherever you want to go. You could go to another country, one you haven't been to before, or you could visit your friends and surprise them by landing in their backyard in your colorfully striped armchair. I doubt that anyone else would have a green and yellow chair like yours that transports you from one place to another.

Feel yourself traveling high in the air, secure on the armchair's seat as it dips and slides to give you a better view of the earth below. There is a button which has "USD" printed there and, if you push it, you will find that you are now upside down. Push "RSU" and you will be then moved to be right side up.

There are waterfalls and waterslides down there. There are parks with swings and climbing frames, and I can see the beach with its lovely golden sand. There are mountain tops with snow on their peaks and, of course, we cannot forget the sky above with its beauty and light.

You can work the controls to take you wherever you want …

The Sun and the Sun God

IN YOUR garden you can smell the lovely perfume that is coming from the golden daffodils nearby. They are standing tall and straight, very proudly sending their aroma to the surrounding trees and flowers.

The air is so fresh and clean, the perfume of the flowers is rich, and the sun a huge golden ball, sending down a very gentle heat. The trees are moving their branches as they welcome the sun's rays. If you listen you can hear them saying, "Come to me, come to me", as they know the sun aids their growth.

Lie down and feel the warmth of the sun on your body, feel it going inside and touching each part of you. It is lovely to feel the sun's light and warmth. It makes you feel good as the rays flicker across your body and the light breeze cools you down.

One of the sun's rays is becoming stronger and stronger, like a beam coming from the core of the sun. In the center of the beam is a sun god who has come down especially to take you up into the heavens, into the sun. Would you like to go? Step into this shaft of light and place your hand into the hand of the sun god and allow yourself to be transported to the sun.

You will feel tranquility around you as you ascend into the heavens and float through the clouds towards the sun, leaving the earth behind.

Isn't it beautiful? Now that you are standing on the sun and feeling its light, you may notice that it has a gentle warmth which enables you to move around freely. You can see the rays of the sun reaching out and touching the earth, bringing its golden light down to the people and the animals and the gardens. It makes the waterfalls and lakes and seas sparkle, and the animals sleepy as they nap, feeling the heat on their fur and feathers.

From where you are, you can see other planets and stars who also receive light from the sun. And if you look a long way away, you will perhaps see other suns and other universes.

This sun god is taking you into the center of the sun, the core of our universe, where his family lives. Perhaps you could stay with them for awhile and find out how they regulate the sun's rays and perhaps you could do it yourself, sending the light out for all those below …

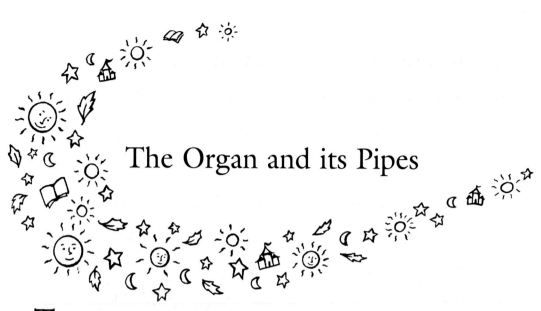

The Organ and its Pipes

THE GREEN of the trees and the grass is very lush, and there are bluebells and roses in pink, mauve and purple. Scattered between these flowers are brilliant yellow daisies moving in the gentle breeze.

Your garden is v-e-r-y quiet, even the trees seem to be standing quietly, not moving a leaf. The animals are hushed, with their ears pricked and the flowers are bending their heads as though they are hearing something you cannot. I wonder what it can be?

Listen carefully, what can you hear? I can hear a heavenly sound of music. It seems to be coming from the direction of the Grandfather Tree. Why don't you go to where he is and see what is happening?

The Grandfather Tree seems to be sheltering a very large object beneath his green branches. It has many keys waiting to be played and many pipes rising up from it, all of different thicknesses and lengths.

It's an organ, the most beautiful organ you have ever heard. There isn't anyone playing it, just the wind which moves across the keyboard and touches the keys so lightly that music pours forth into your garden.

The music seems to be attracting everybody to sit and listen. The clearing is rapidly filling up with animals, fairies and elves. The birds are flying in to nestle on the branches and their babies are chirping softly in unison with the music.

What would you like to do? You could sit quietly in the clearing listening to the organ music, or perhaps you may want to play the organ yourself.

Grandfather Tree is smiling as though to himself, and one of his long leafy arms is beckoning you to come and sit on the small seat in front of the organ. He would like you to play.

Why don't you try? Sit on the seat and it will adjust itself to the right height for you. The pipes are very tall and imposing.

The organ has many knobs for you to move to co-ordinate the sounds that will come through these pipes. Just alter a few and test the keyboard for the sound, and then readjust the knobs until you get the sound which is right for you.

And now you are ready to play. The organ music is pouring forth, surrounding your garden and filling it with the joy that this music is bringing. All the little ones, who have come to listen in your garden, love hearing you play and are swaying to the music. Indeed a few of them have decided to dance.

You don't need the sheet of music in front of you as the music itself seems to be in your blood and comes forth from your fingertips.

You can change the tune as many times as you want. Play a medley perhaps, or something nice and quiet. It is up to you …

The Submarine

FEEL THE freshness of the grass and the dew beneath your feet as you go forward into your garden. Breathe in the aroma from the flowers' perfume drifting towards you on the light breeze. The powdery clouds drift high in the velvet blue of the sky, making intricate patterns.

The sun is sending down a lovely warm glow which settles over your garden. The trees and the flowers love the feel of the sun's warmth which helps them to grow. As you walk down the pathway, you can hear the sound of water. I wonder where it is coming from? If you go a little further, you will come to your special beach.

The sand is a golden yellow and it crunches beneath your feet, gleaming in the light of the sun. The sea gulls swoop over the iridescent blue water, dipping over the waves as they roll to the shore. Small sand crabs make their way towards the nearby rocks to shelter in the small pools of water that have formed there.

There are some boats moored off the shore that stand in relief against the skyline. Some of them have the rigging of the old schooners that went to sea in days gone by and others are modern and sleek, shining in the sun.

Why don't you run down the beach and throw yourself into the waves which are lapping quietly on the sand? And then let the water take you out to where these boats are resting. You could swim there or you could lie on your back and let the waves carry you, going gently up and down, until you reach these magnificent tall boats.

As you look at the schooners, you will notice another type of boat nearby. It looks something like a very large cigar with a tower that moves, searching the horizon like the eyes of this craft. Why, it is a submarine with its periscope.

Have you been on a submarine before? See, someone is climbing out from the top of the submarine and waving to you. It must be the captain wanting you to join him. It is fun going down into the depths of this vessel, very different to being on a normal boat.

You can operate the periscope, watching from underneath the water what is going on above, or you can pull it down as they close all the hatches, and then take off for the deeper part of the sea.

There are many things to see on a submarine — where the men sleep in bunks above each other, and where they eat. Their kitchen is very compact and complete and their food is always fresh and delightful.

Perhaps the captain of the submarine would let you operate the submarine. You could take it deep, deep down within the waters, to places where you would not normally go. You can watch the fish swimming by — large ones, small ones. Look, there's a shark! And, there — an octopus. Oh, there are so many things you can do and see on the submarine …

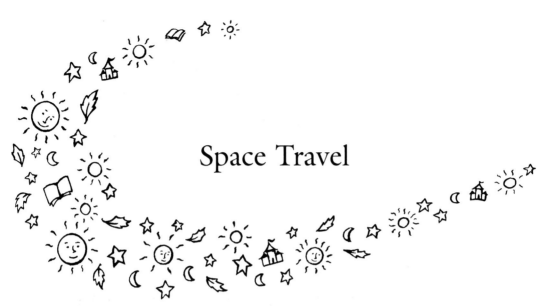

Space Travel

I WANT you to walk along the garden path, feeling the sun on your back. The gentle breeze is ruffling your hair as you climb to the top of a hill. When you stand on the top of this hill you can see far, far away, as far as the eye can see.

How wonderful it would be to travel through space, to feel effortless and to feel timeless. There are

many different ways you could travel through space.
One way perhaps might be by putting a rocket on
your back and saying "lift off" — or perhaps having
your own space vehicle — or perhaps by just
"wishing" that you were there.

This time, why don't you have your own space
craft and then you can navigate the airship? You could
wear a space suit made of silver material, which has
threads of purple woven through it. Your shoes have
a heavier sole than normal which will help you to
jump from one rock to another, or one surface to
another when you land. There is no need for a
helmet, unless you want, as you will be able to
breathe the air in space without difficulty. You may
want to wear a hat of some kind, perhaps one which

comes to a peak high above your head, made of purple with silver threads, and a purple visor to keep any glare from your eyes.

You are now at the controls. There are many buttons and levers but you seem to know which ones to push and press. There is one there that says "push for lift off" — and you have, you have lifted off the surface of the earth.

Your space machine is taking you quickly into outer space, leaving the earth dimension behind. It is so very beautiful; the stars are huge and, look, there is the moon luminescent and golden against the velvet black sky. You could go to the far side of the moon, if you like, as no one from earth has been there before, or you could go towards the sun.

If you take your craft completely around the sun, you will feel a different energy from that of the moon's circle.

Why don't you go further afield to see what other worlds exist? Move the throttle forward as you go into a timelessness that you haven't experienced before and, look, there are planets whirling by. You are going into other galaxies and other times and other worlds.

How exciting to be able to travel like this, to have this freedom. Where would you like to land? On a star? On a new planet? I wonder if anyone lives on these stars and planets. Why don't you move the throttle slowly and maneuver your craft downward onto the planet or world or star you have decided to visit. You need have no fear because wherever you land or wherever you go, you will find people who are going to welcome you and take you into their worlds.

Feel yourself emerging from your craft and investigating, investigating, going where no one from earth has been …

The Geese, the Ducks
and the Swans

As YOU enter your garden, you hear the flowers
talking to each other and the grass growing. The
grass is soft underneath your feet and it springs back
to life as you walk forward. The bees are going from
flower to flower, and the fairies and elves dance in the
clearing.

You feel the warmth of the sun caressing you and the light breeze moves your hair softly. You can hear the birds calling to each other. There is nothing in your garden which can harm you, each and every creature lives in harmony with the others.

I want you to feel the peace that is flowing in your garden and the gentleness of all who live there. Your path is winding through the trees and it will take you to a beautiful lake surrounded by weeping willows, whose long fingers dangle in the water and move to and fro with its motion.

There is a small table set up, with an umbrella to shade you from the sun. There are sandwiches and drinks on the table, plus a few loaves of bread. I wonder why the bread is there?

Put your feet up and enjoy being by the lake watching the water. You will see, if you look closely, that there are eels swimming under its surface, and many golden fish darting among the reeds.

And look over there, a gaggle of geese are coming across the grass to join you. Aren't they funny with their swaying walk on their webbed feet?

But I hear a different sound than the geese. Listen to it — quack, quack, quack. On the lake there are ducks quacking loudly as they head towards you, happy that you are there.

If you look to the other side of the lake, you will notice that the swans are also swimming very majestically towards where you are sitting.

Now you know why you have the bread. It must be feeding time. Break some bread off and spread it around in front of you. This will encourage the birds to come out of the water and eat with you. The geese are picking up the small pieces of bread before the ducks and the swans can get there. You had better save some for them.

I wonder if some of them have names? Why don't you make up a few names and call to them? And then they will come close enough for you to feed them by hand. They will love being fed by you and they are going to make many noises as they eat. Perhaps it is now time to open the other loaf of bread …

The Four Winds

AS YOU enter your garden, you become aware of the softness of the air caressing your cheeks, and the warmth of the sun on your body. Look around and you can see the trees and plants all happily sharing the same earth with the flowers and the animals.

The sky is a deep shade of blue and the golden sun is high in the heavens, warming the earth and all of its creatures.

The path in front of you is winding along through the soft dewy grass and up onto a hill which isn't difficult to climb.

Standing on the crest of the hill, you feel the light breeze sweeping around your body and becoming stronger. This breeze is whispering to you that he is becoming one with the Westerly Wind and that, if you want, the Westerly Wind will take you to where all the winds are going to meet.

Allow the wind to wrap his energy around you and to transport you forward. Can you feel this wind's strength as he takes you to meet the winds that are coming from all directions?

Look, the Northerly Wind is approaching and she is smiling as she sweeps and dips, cavorting like a young lamb. She is going to take you by the hand to the northern part of your garden so that you can see from above what happens there. Can you see your home? Or perhaps your school?

The Easterly Wind is gently approaching and is sweeping around you as she speaks with the Northerly Wind. They are wondering where the Southerly Wind is. Oh, there he is. He has met up with the Westerly Wind and they are both sweeping in to meet with the other winds and yourself.

As they all come together, they are going to send out a big breath which is going to tumble you over and over, up into the air, and then down again. This is fun and the winds laugh as they blow you gently up and down.

You could go with the winds and experience how it feels to be with them as they blow across the fields, bending the corn and the flowers as they pass over. You would feel what it would be like to move through the leaves on the trees and to ruffle the feathers on the birds and the fur on the animals.

As the winds swoop over the deserts, the sand will swirl and move into the air. The winds can whip up the sea's waves, causing droplets of water to fly in all directions.

There is a large white cloud overhead and perhaps you could be blown onto it. Why don't you ask the winds if they would gently breathe on you and send you onto the soft whiteness of this cloud …

The Horses

FEEL THE freshness of the air surrounding you, caressing your skin and stirring your hair as though gentle fingers are moving it. In your garden there are snapdragons in all their pretty colors and the green grass beneath your feet feels like velvet. The tall trees are bending slightly in the breeze that ruffles their branches, and the perfume from the roses drifts around you.

There seems to be something happening in your garden. There are bags of sugar by your feet and I can hear all sorts of sounds and there are different smells around also. Listen! There are sounds like thunder rolling towards you.

Coming towards you is a herd of horses. They are so beautiful as they take long strides in your direction. They are being led by not one, but two horses, each quite different than the other. One is jet black and the other as white as the driven snow.

They are before you now, standing on their back legs and pawing the air as though to greet you. They are coming down to the earth now and moving forward for you to pat their necks and caress their manes.

The herd is coming to rest behind them. Some of them are brown with white markings and others are piebald. Some are white with dashes of brown and black. And there are some with shy foals beside them.

The horses are all milling around, wanting to come closer for you to pat them. The two leaders again rear onto their hind legs and whinny strongly, as though to tell their followers that they can now approach you.

Pick up one of the bags of sugar and give one piece to each horse. For the foals, you could perhaps break each piece into two.

Doesn't it feel nice to have them nuzzling the sugar from your outstretched hand? You can pat each one behind their ears or stroke their noses. Their eyes are large and bright and each horse has utter trust and faith in you.

Would you like to choose one to ride? You could ride first the black one for a time and then change to the white one, or perhaps you may prefer one of the piebald ponies.

There is no need for a saddle. Swing yourself onto the back of the horse you have chosen and feel the horse breaking from a walk to a trot, to a canter, to a gallop. Feel the wind whistling past your face as your horse takes you flying across the earth, its feet landing safely and securely each time.

Your horse is now slowing to a halt as there is a stream ahead which is shaded by low-slung trees. It is time for the herd to rest and to drink from these cool waters.

You can slide down from your horse and perhaps you could play with the foals for a time …

Also by Maureen Garth

Driven by the desire to help her three-year-old daughter settle down to a peaceful night's sleep, Maureen Garth devised meditations that would help her daughter feel secure and cared for. *Starbright*, Maureen Garth's first book, is a collection of the stories she created as her child grew older. These innovative meditations are simple visualizations parents and teachers can read to their children to help them sleep, to help them develop their concentration, to help them awaken their creativity, and to help them learn to quiet themselves.

"Unfortunately, a lot of children have trouble learning these techniques by the time they are seven or eight," writes Garth. "Relaxation and visualization, if taught at an earlier age, could enhance not only children's school work but other areas of their lives. Their concentration would improve; their artistic abilities would develop; they would feel more centered; their daydreaming could not only bring joy, but be constructive."

In her engaging, warm, and personal style, Garth teaches parents and other carers how to help their children relax, concentrate, and develop their artistic and mental abilities, as well as how to help them enjoy a good night's sleep.

CollinsDove
An imprint of HarperCollins*Publishers*

ISBN 1 86371 206 2

Also by Maureen Garth

Maureen Garth's first collection of meditations for children, *Starbright*, attracted an immediate world-wide response from parents, teachers and the children themselves.

This second collection of children's stories, *Moonbeam*, will further help children to learn meditation from an early age. They will find their concentration improved, their creative abilities enhanced, and their capacity to deal with anxieties strengthened.

Maureen Garth shows parents how to use these imaginings with their children and to discover unsuspected benefits both for the children and for themselves.

"Nurturing in children a sense that they are never alone, that they are in loving company always, and can always find that caring presence in their hearts, may be the most subtle but precious gift we can bestow on them. These simple exercises, with their straightforward, gentle language, helped this concerned parent begin to do just that."

Phil Catalfo, *New Dimensions*

CollinsDove
An imprint of HarperCollins*Publishers*

ISBN 1 86371 142 2

Also by Maureen Garth

Meditation can give us the strength, purpose and direction we need in our lives. It can make us more conscious of our surroundings, more aware of people and their needs, more tolerant of others.

In *The Inner Garden*, Maureen Garth, best-selling author of the *Starbright* and *Moonbeam* collections of meditations for children, has now written a set of creative visualizations for all ages. Garth's innovative way of leading the reader into the "gentle art of going within" results in a book that offers help in many situations.

The Inner Garden introduces an enjoyable and freeing technique that is simple to follow and points to a rich source of inner experience. There are visualizations for healing the mind and the body, for acquiring confidence, for relaxation, for improving concentration, and to quieten fears and aid sleep.

"In *The Inner Garden*, Maureen Garth has used her wonderful imagination to develop a series of creative visualization exercises. This particular form of meditation will help many people to escape from the pressures of daily life and to find a new level of ease and comfort, health and wellbeing. Appealing to both young and old, this book could well be an effective step on your own path to inner peace."

Ian Gawler,
author of *Peace of Mind* and *You Can Conquer Cancer.*

CollinsDove
An imprint of HarperCollins*Publishers*

ISBN 1 86371 329 8